I0489244

THIS BOOK BELONGS TO

. . . .

AT THE CROSS

Color for the Soul

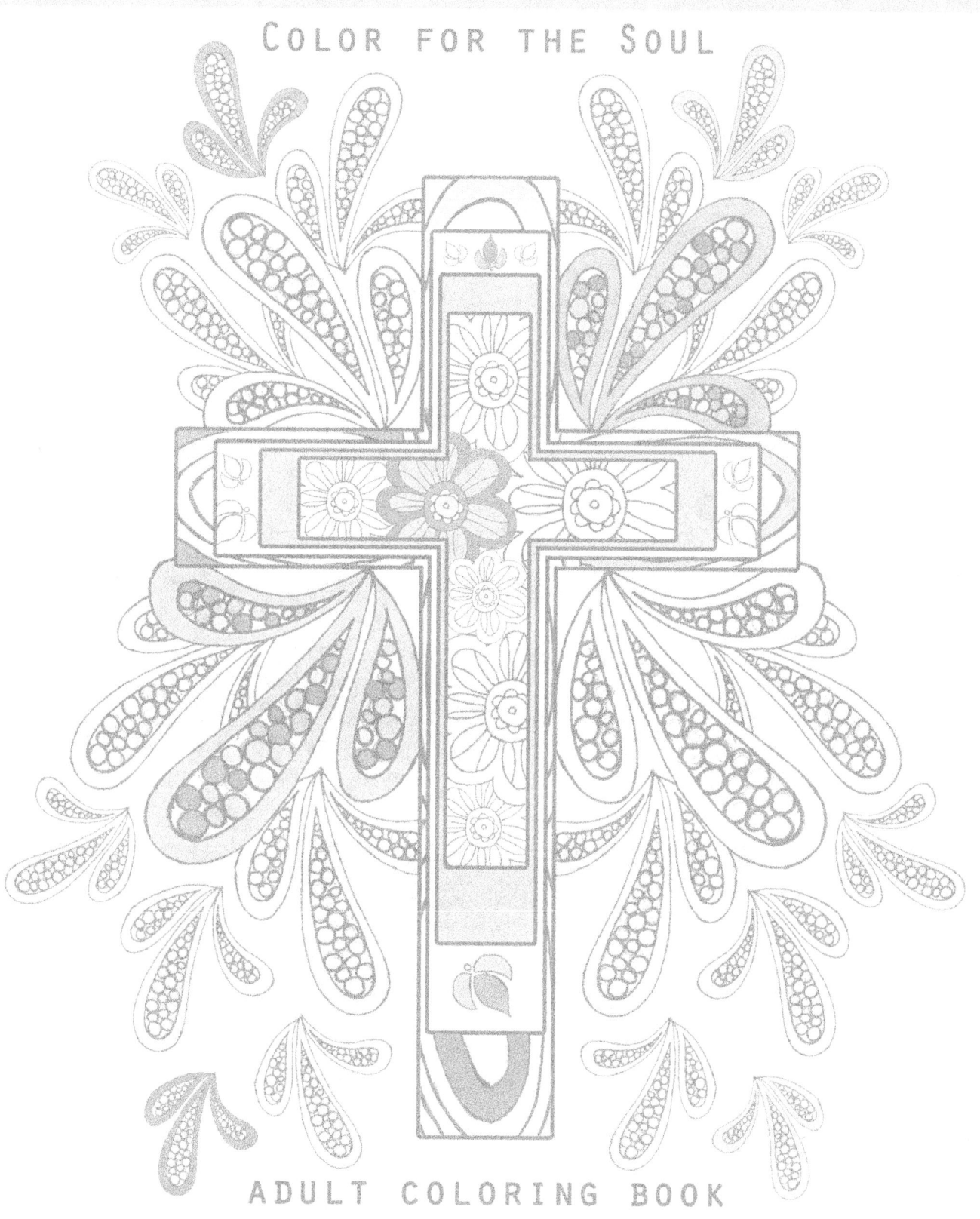

ADULT COLORING BOOK

T.S. DOBSON

AT THE CROSS
COLOR FOR THE SOUL

an Adult Coloring Book

Copyright 2015 by Teresa Scott Dobson (author of The Fruit of the Spirit: For Preteens; The Twelve Outlaws: A Disciple Bible Study for Teens; Pocketful of Faith, Hope, and Love, Pocketful of Prayers and The Fruit of the Spirit: Adult Coloring Journal).

ISBN-13: 978-1522773979
ISBN-10: 1522773975

Cover and Interior Art by Teresa Scott Dobson

Editor: Matthew Dobson (author of the Living With Purpose series: Volume 1 & 2; Authentic Teenager: A Life Study for Teens; Spiritual Warfare, Understanding the Higher Power, and Running With Purpose)

All rights reserved.

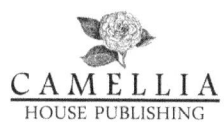

CAMELLIA
HOUSE PUBLISHING

Camellia House Publishing, Century, FL
Printed in the United States of America.

camelliahousepublishing@aol.com

Before You Get Started!

1. Put away all of the worldly distractions around you -- TV, phone, computer, etc. Get alone with God!

2. Take out some color pencils, markers or crayons.

3. Pick a page and go with it. There's no particular order to follow. Let God's Spirit guide you. Practice meditating on God and cast away your worry, stress, fear, and anxiety.

4. When you finish a design, personalize it by signing your name anywhere on the page.

5. Find the drawing pad in the back of the book and doodle your own cross designs then color them!

6. Stop when you need a break, then pick it up again later.

7. When finished, if you desire, share your creations with others!

8. One more thing...try and look for the optical illusion of movement in one of the Crosses!

We would love to see any of your finished creations! Send a picture of your art to

camelliahousepublishing@aol.com

(Attach png or jpeg files 10 megs or less per email)

24 Then Jesus said to his disciples, "Whoever wants to be my disciple must deny themselves and take up their cross and follow me. 25 For whoever wants to save their life will lose it, but whoever loses their life for me will find it. 26 What good will it be for someone to gain the whole world, yet forfeit their soul? Or what can anyone give in exchange for their soul?"

Matthew 16:24-26 (NIV)

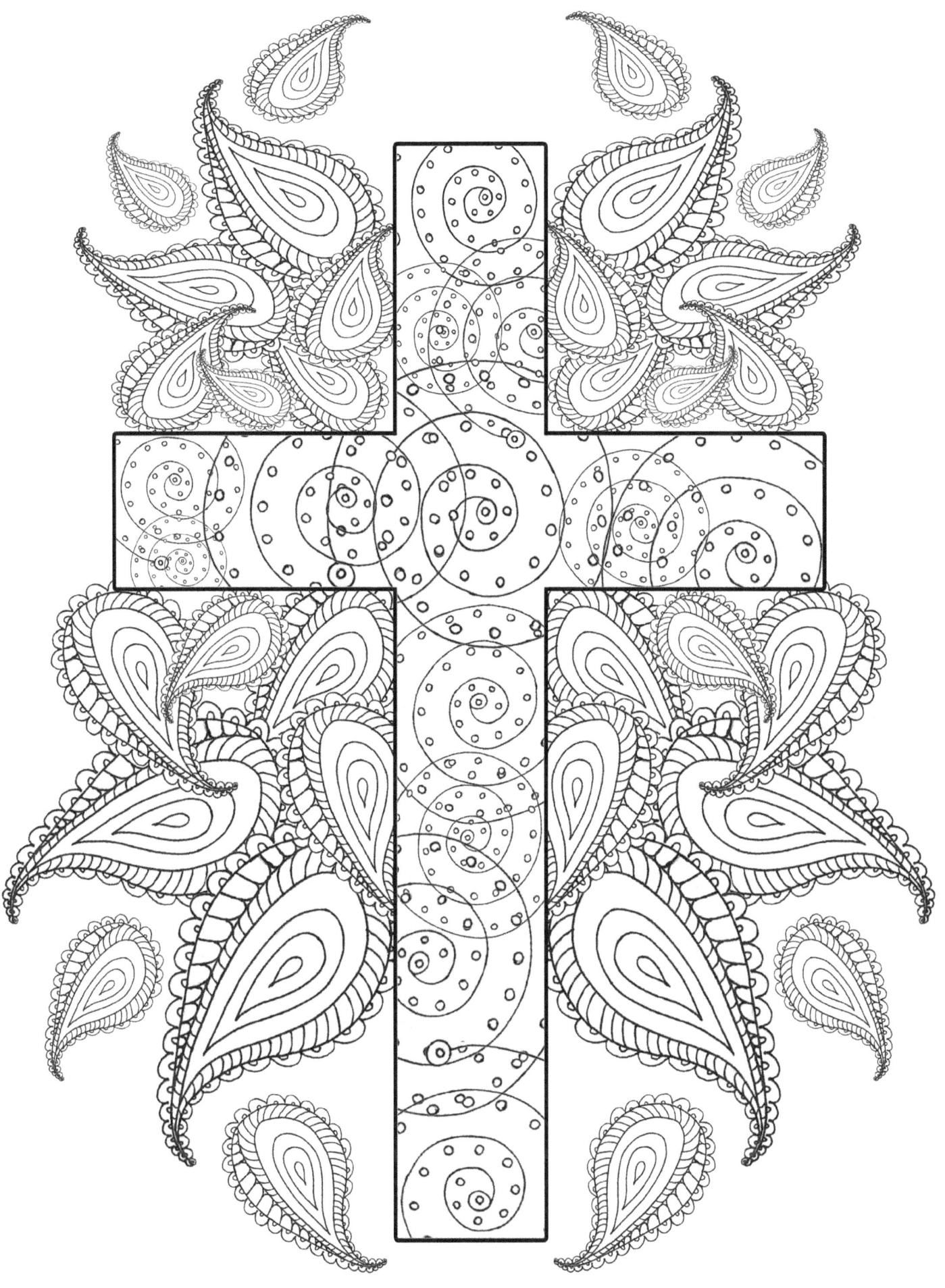

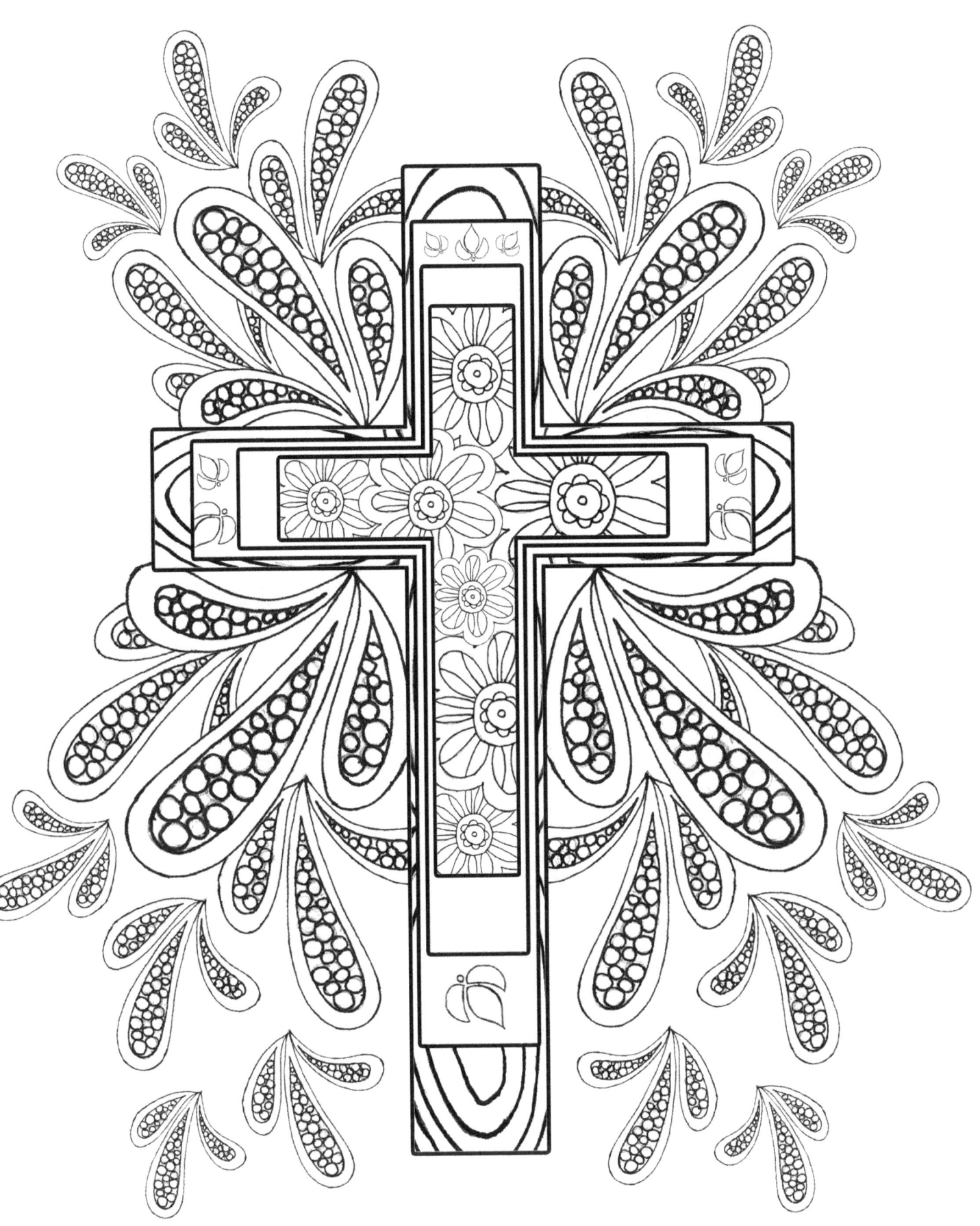

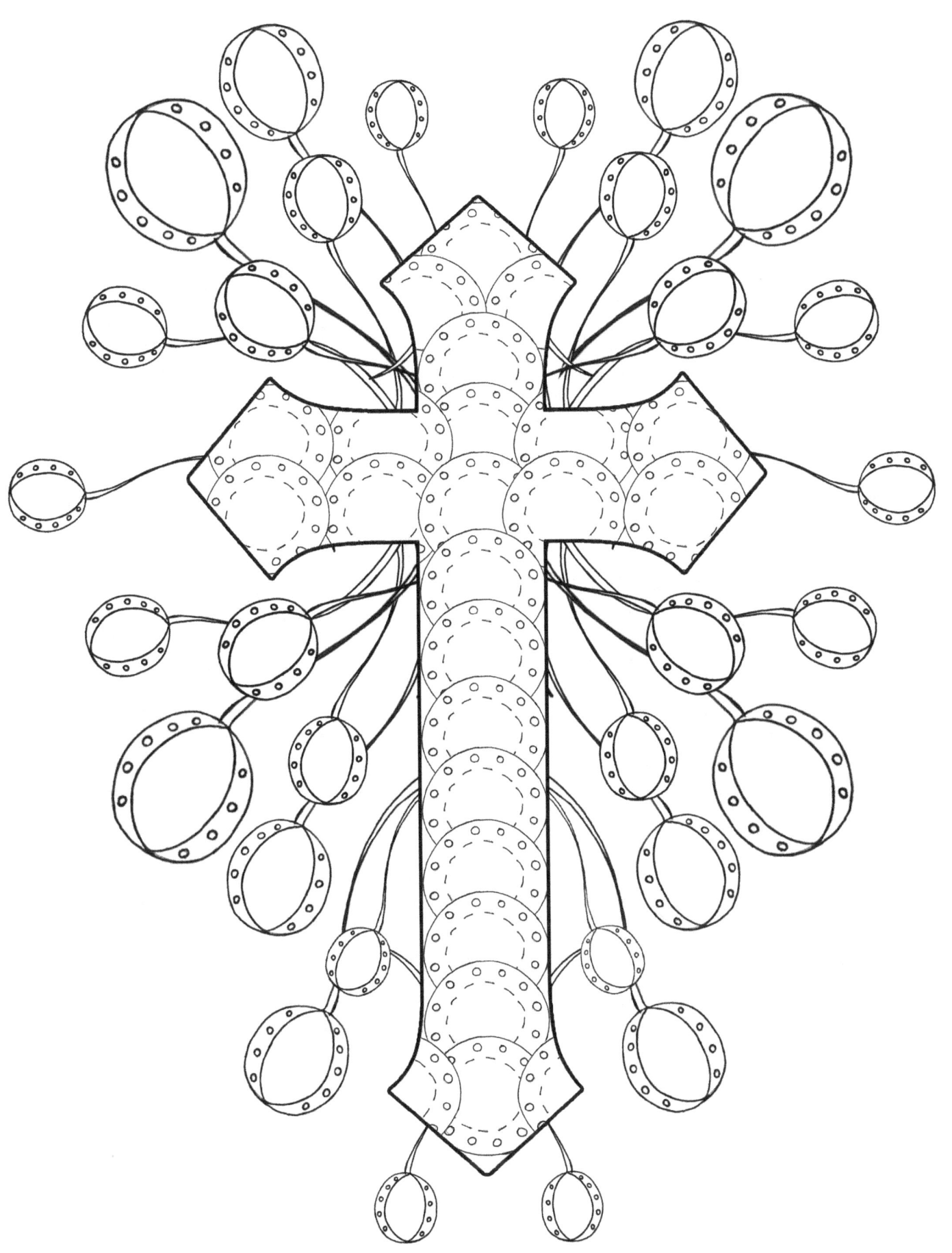

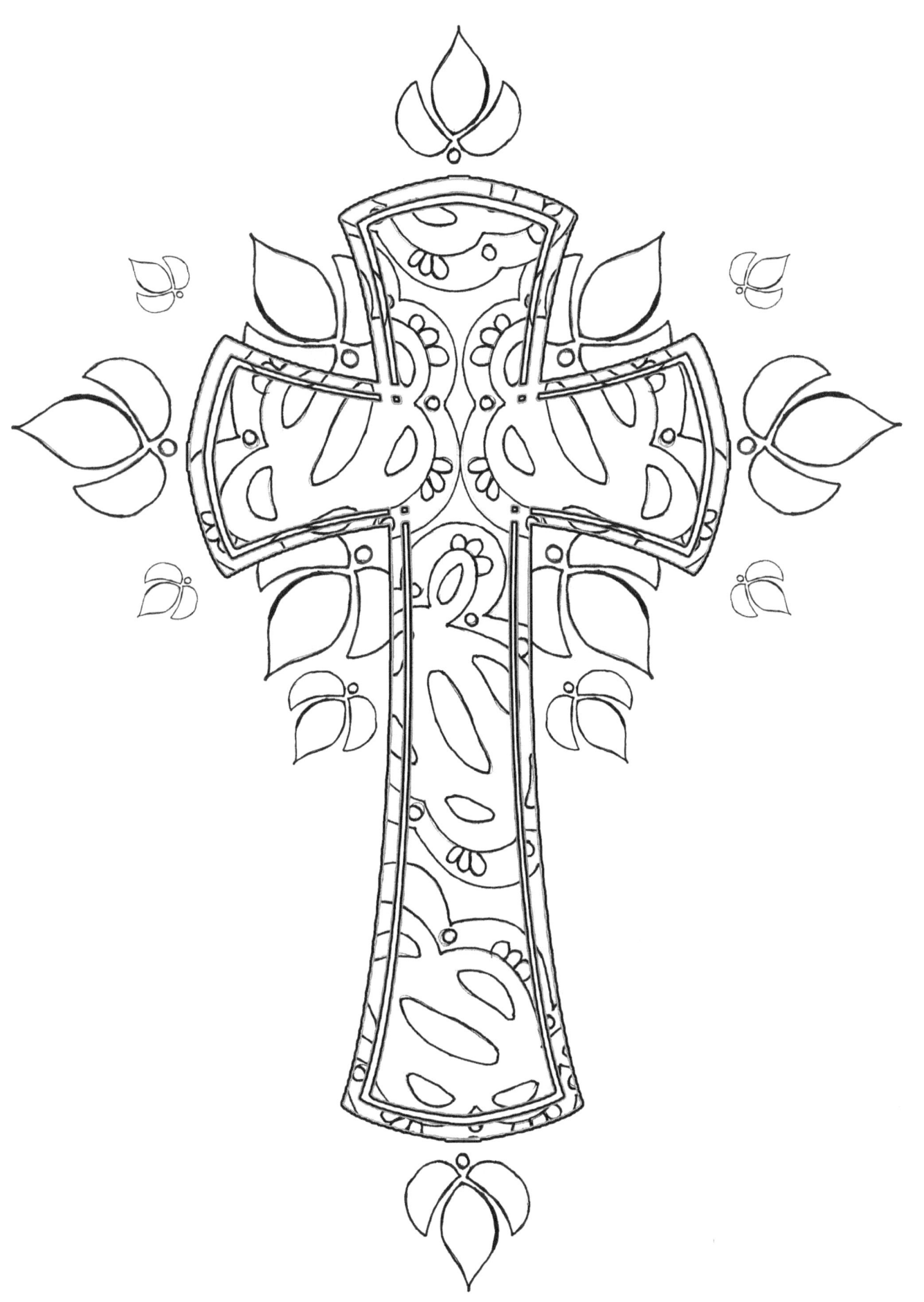

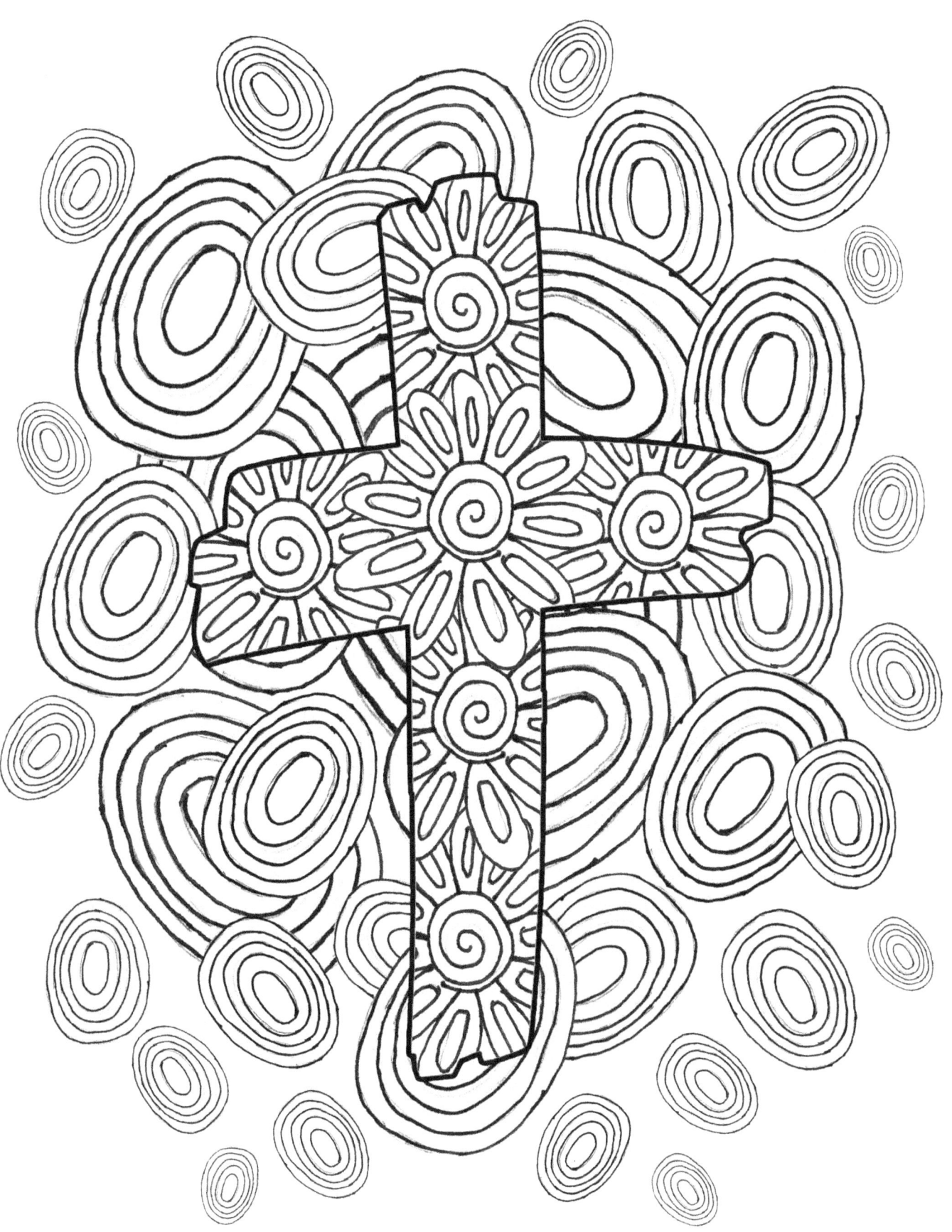

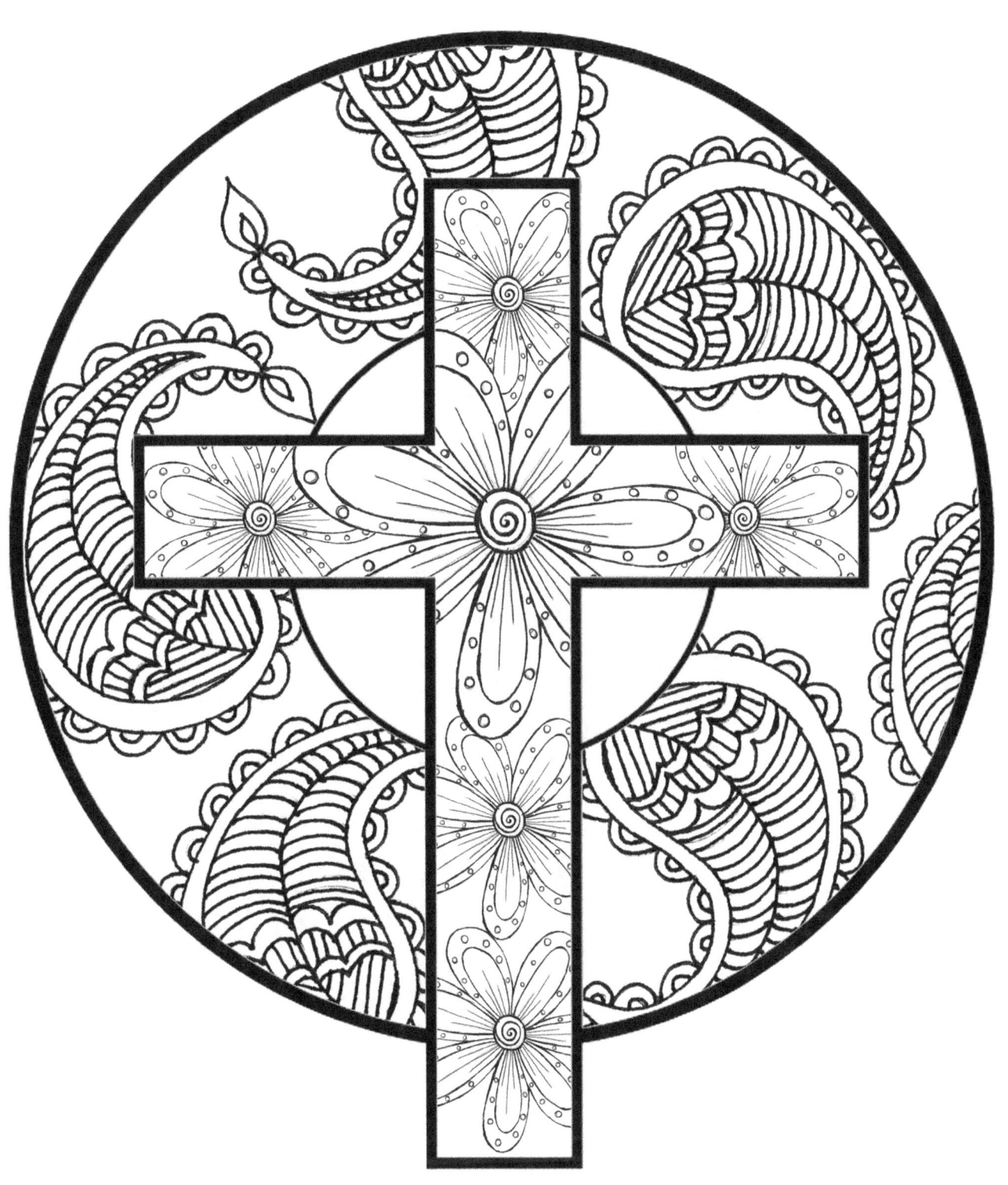

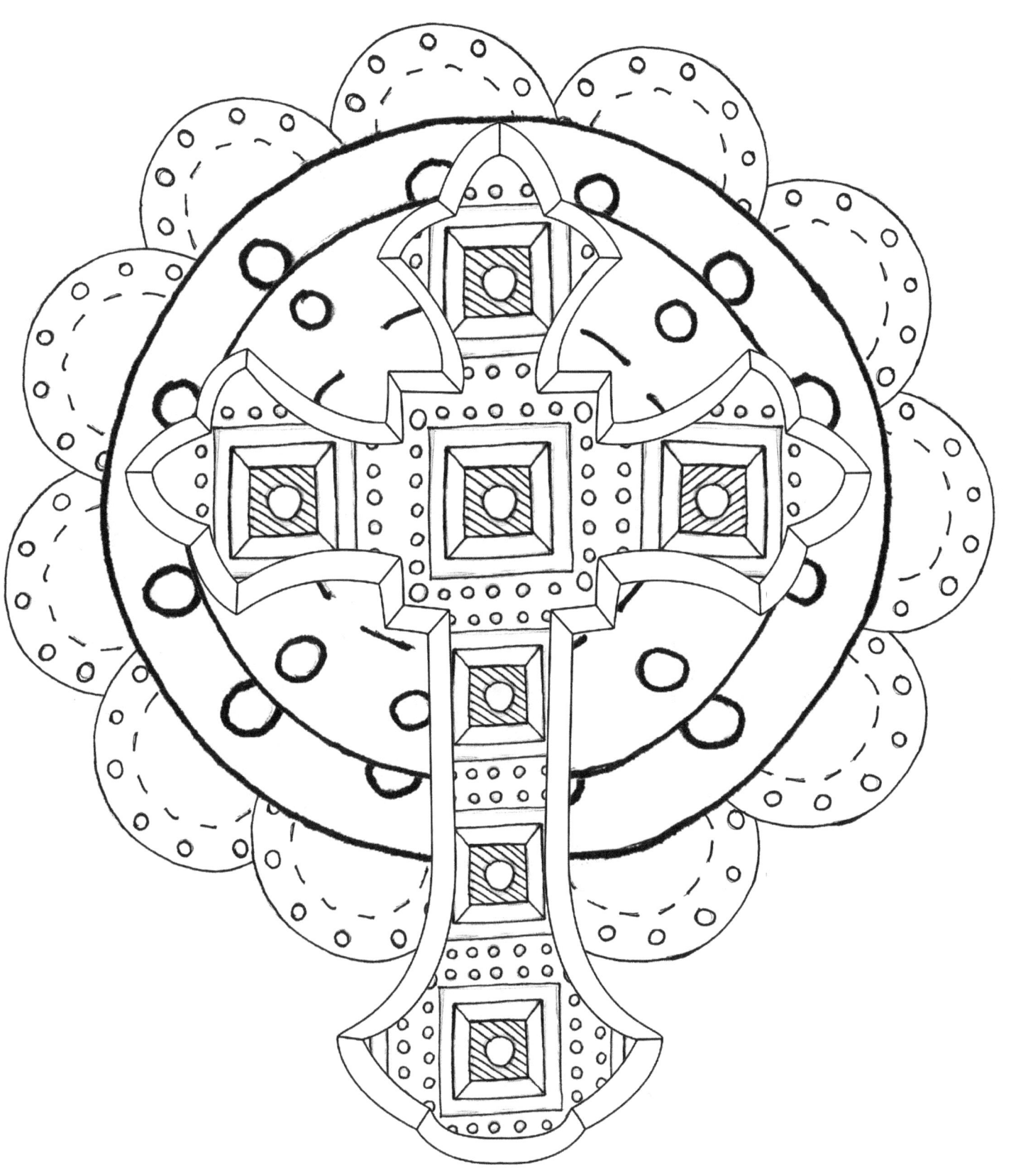

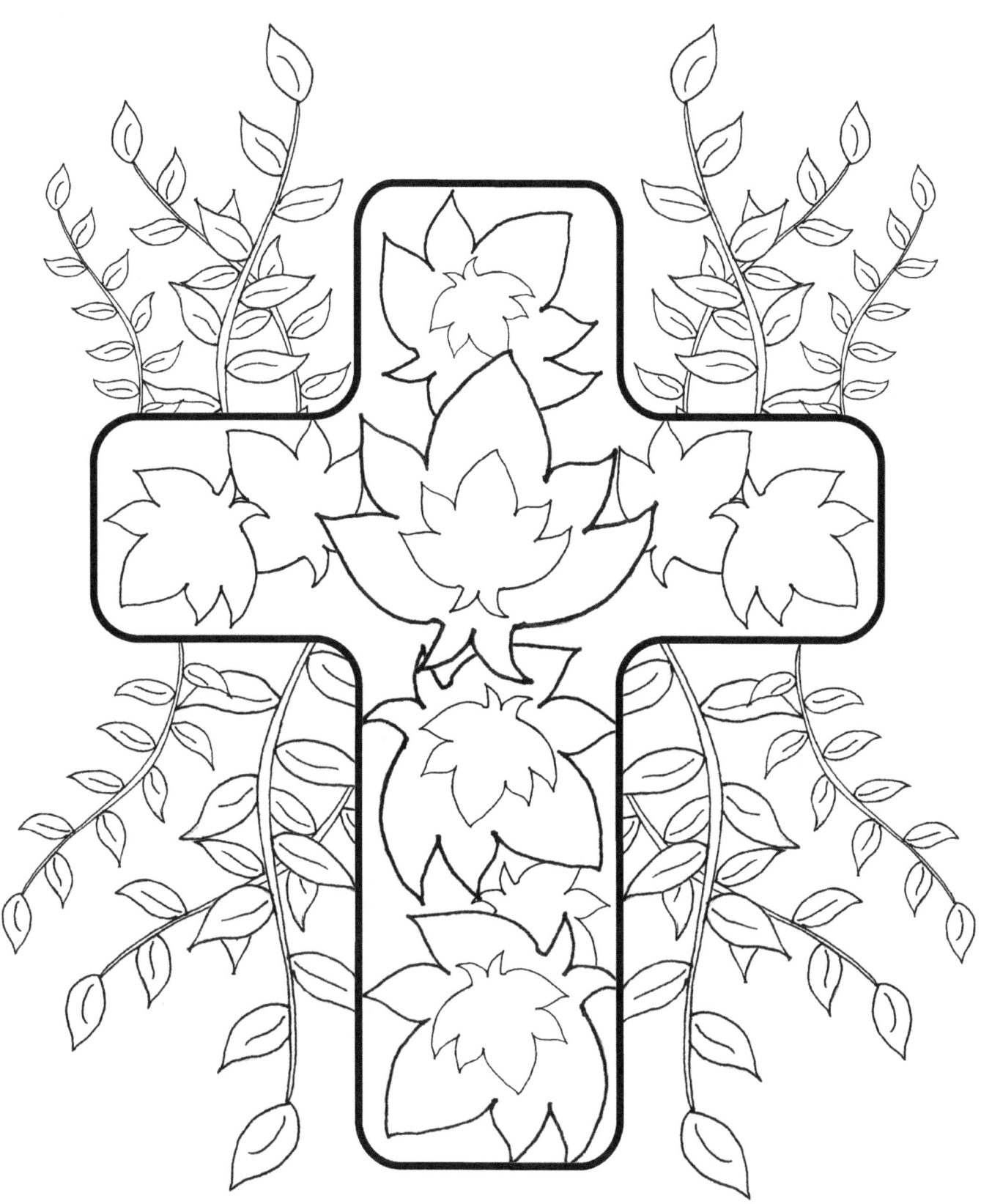

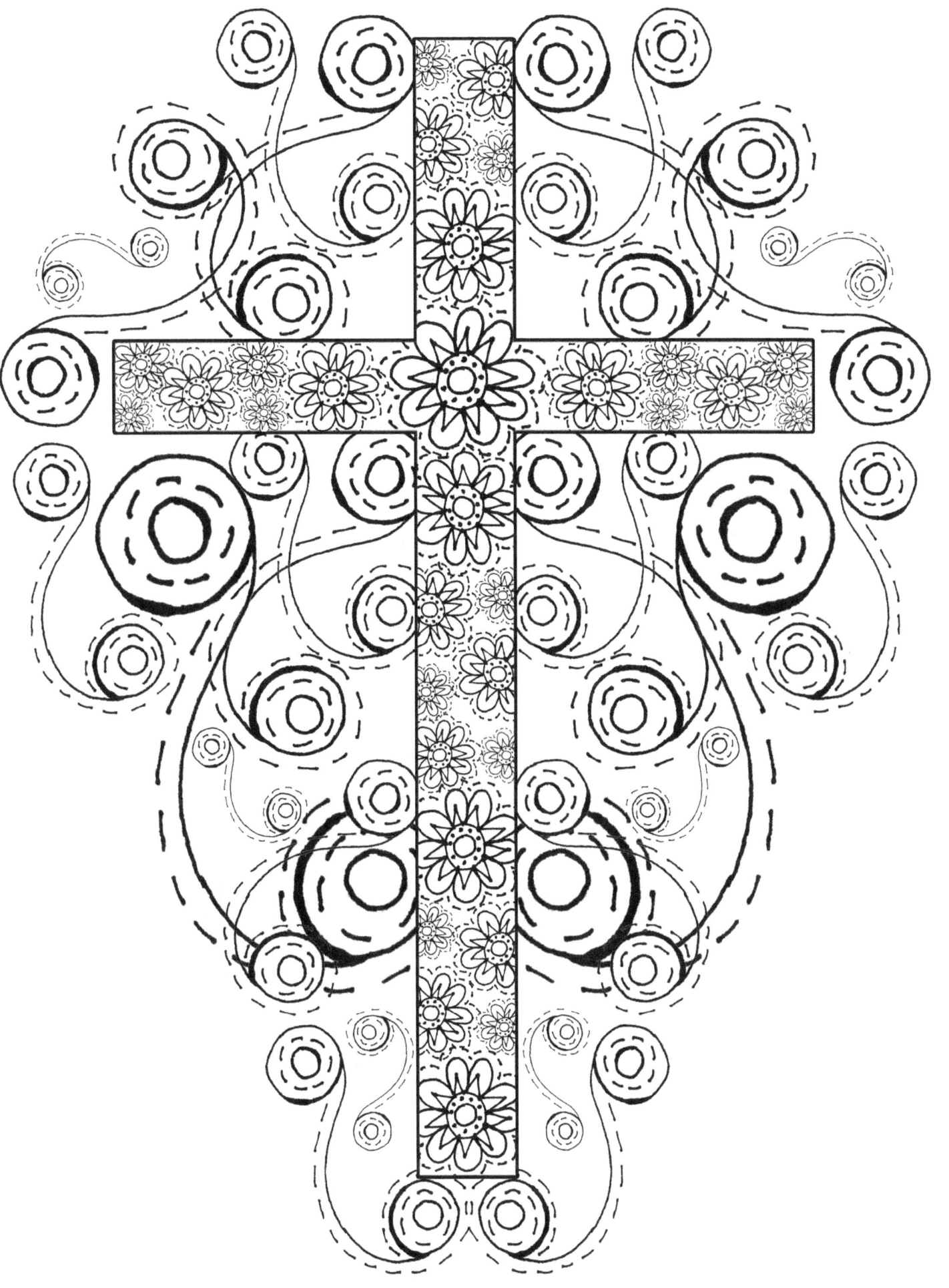

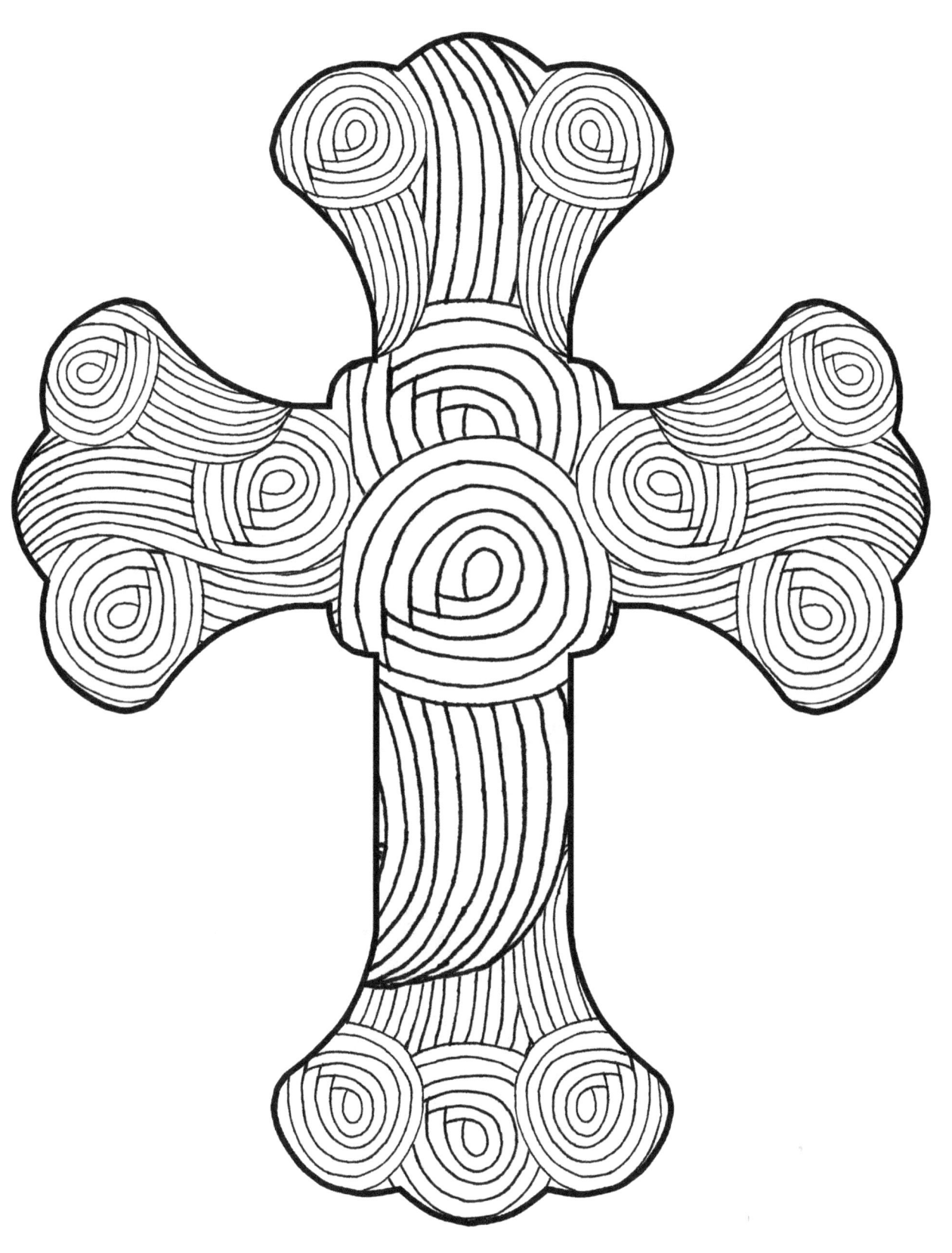

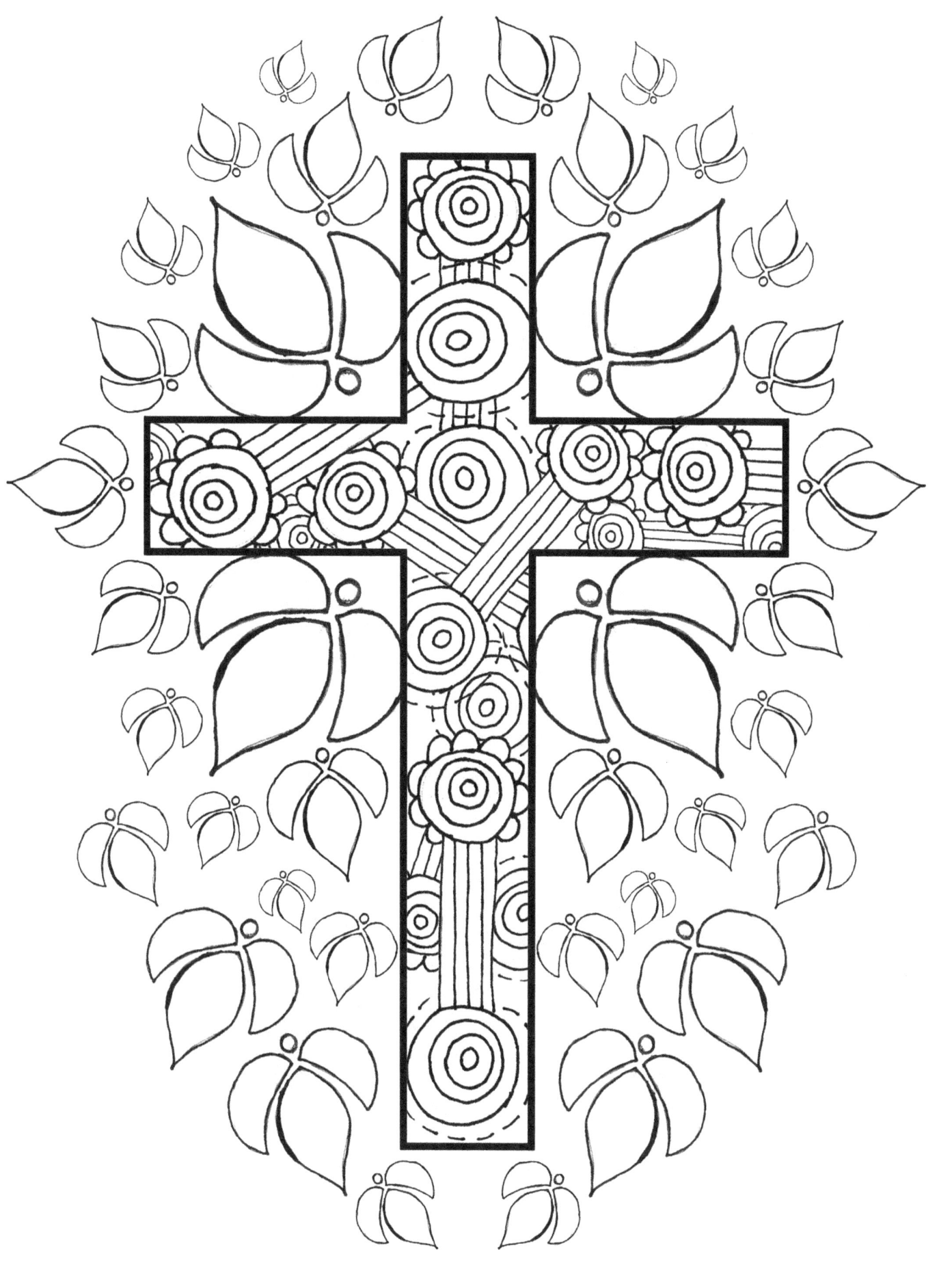

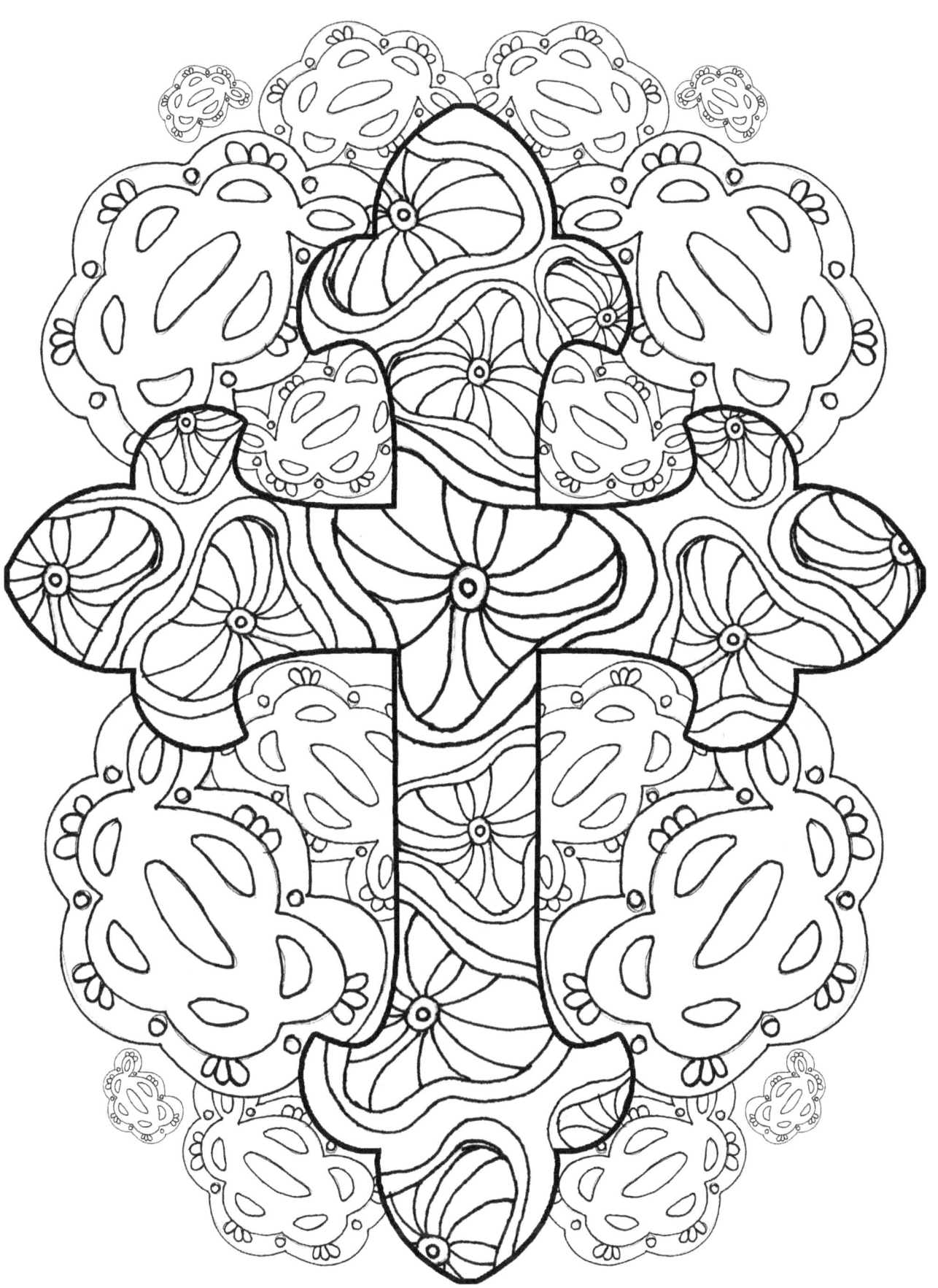

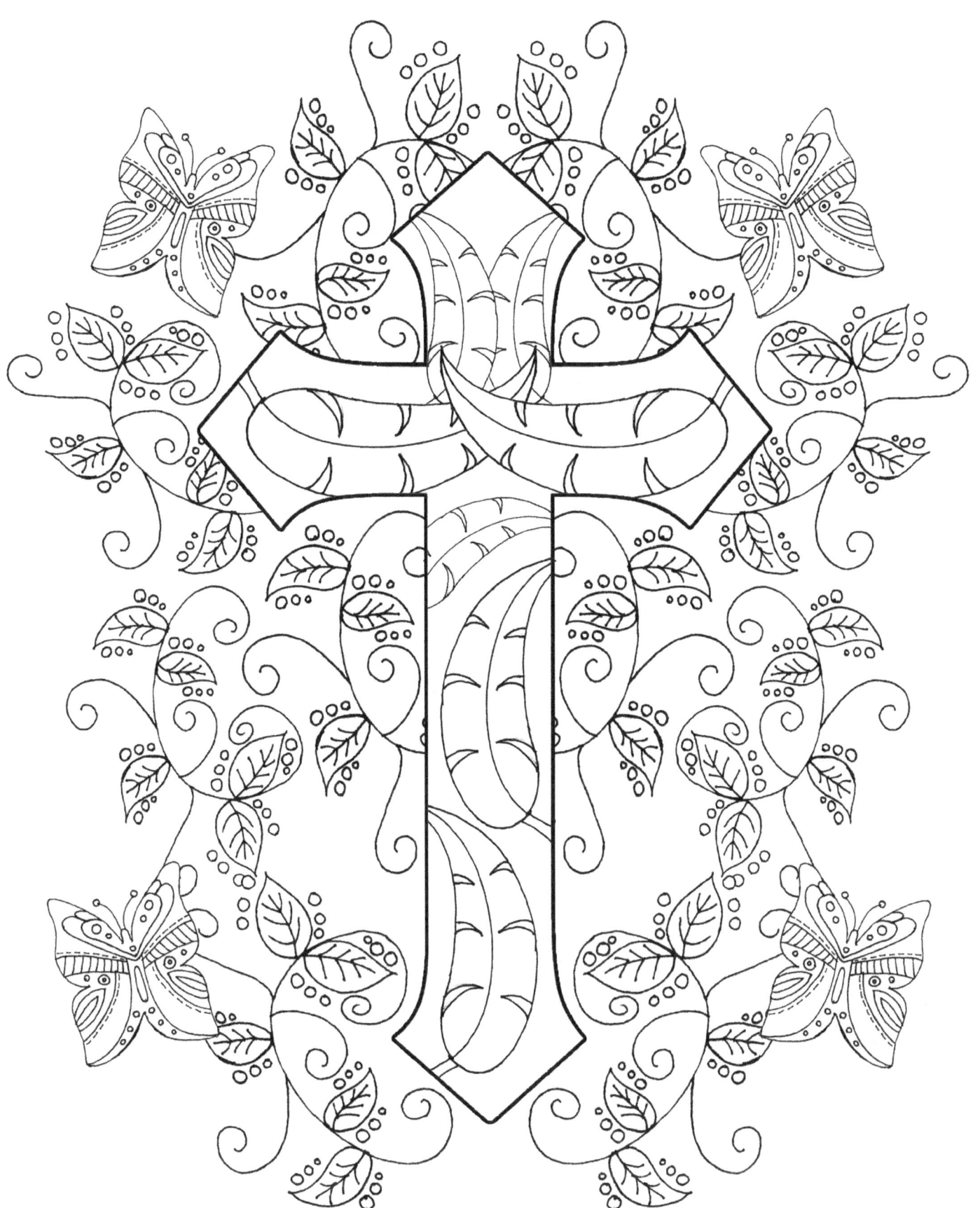

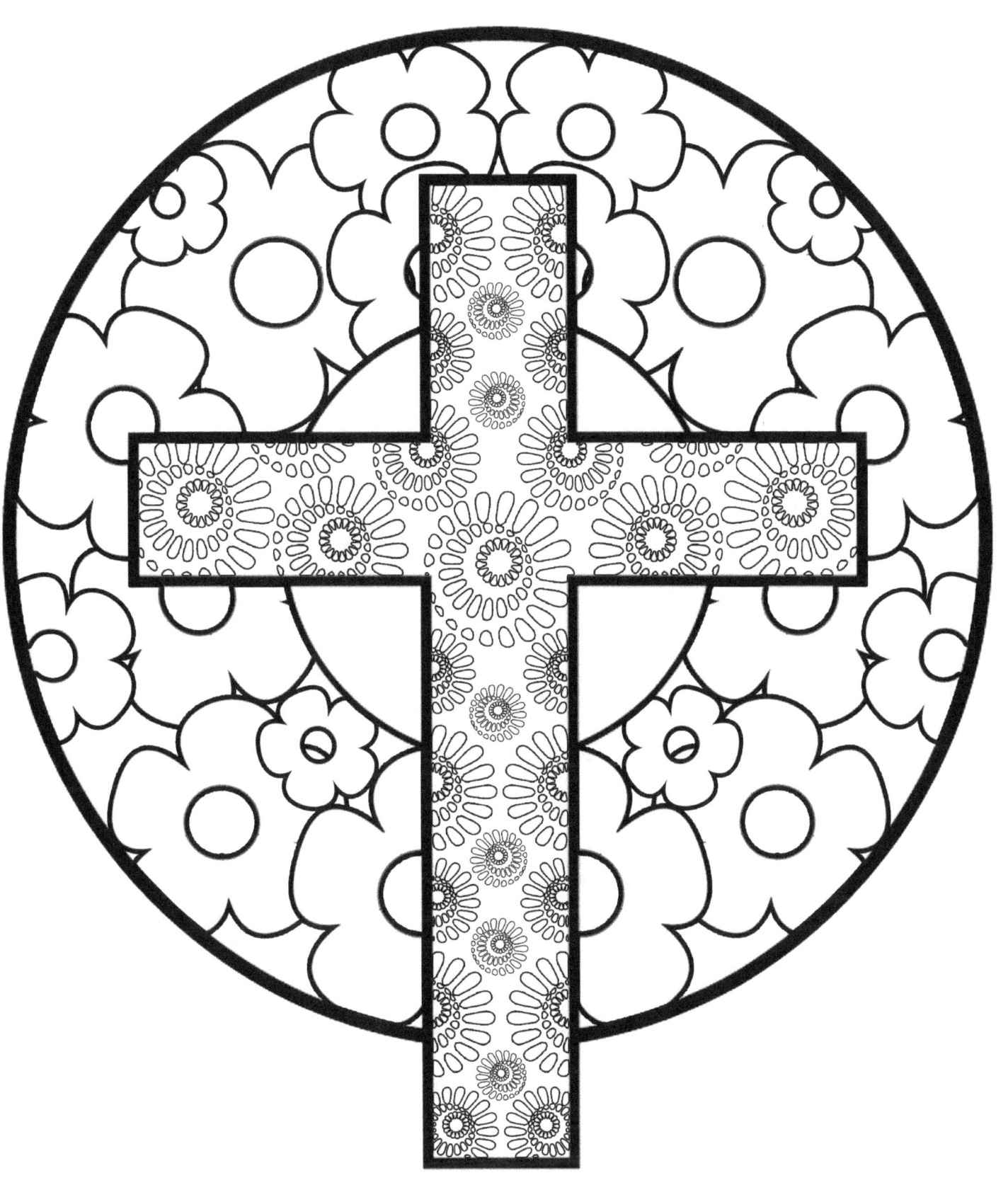

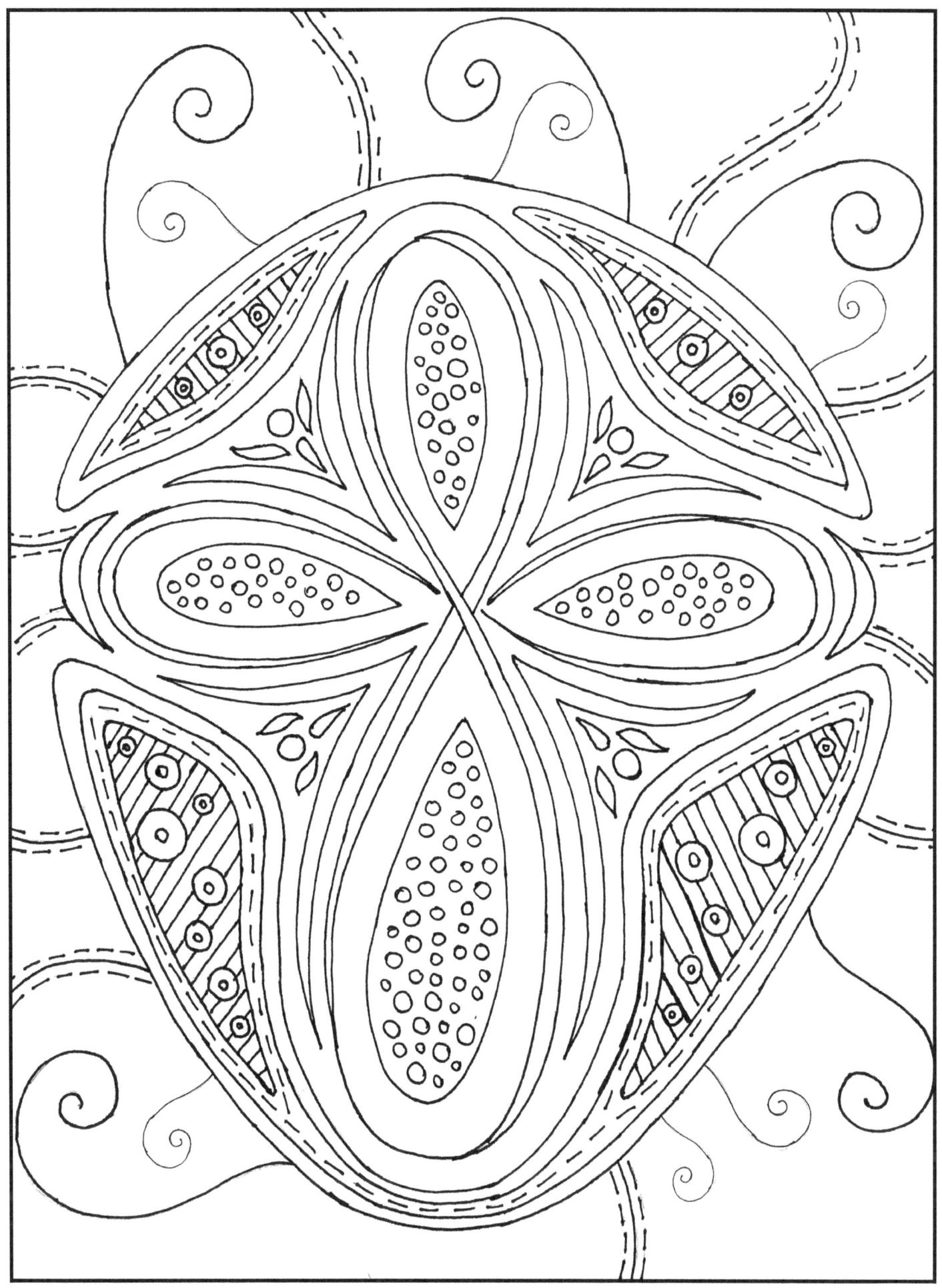

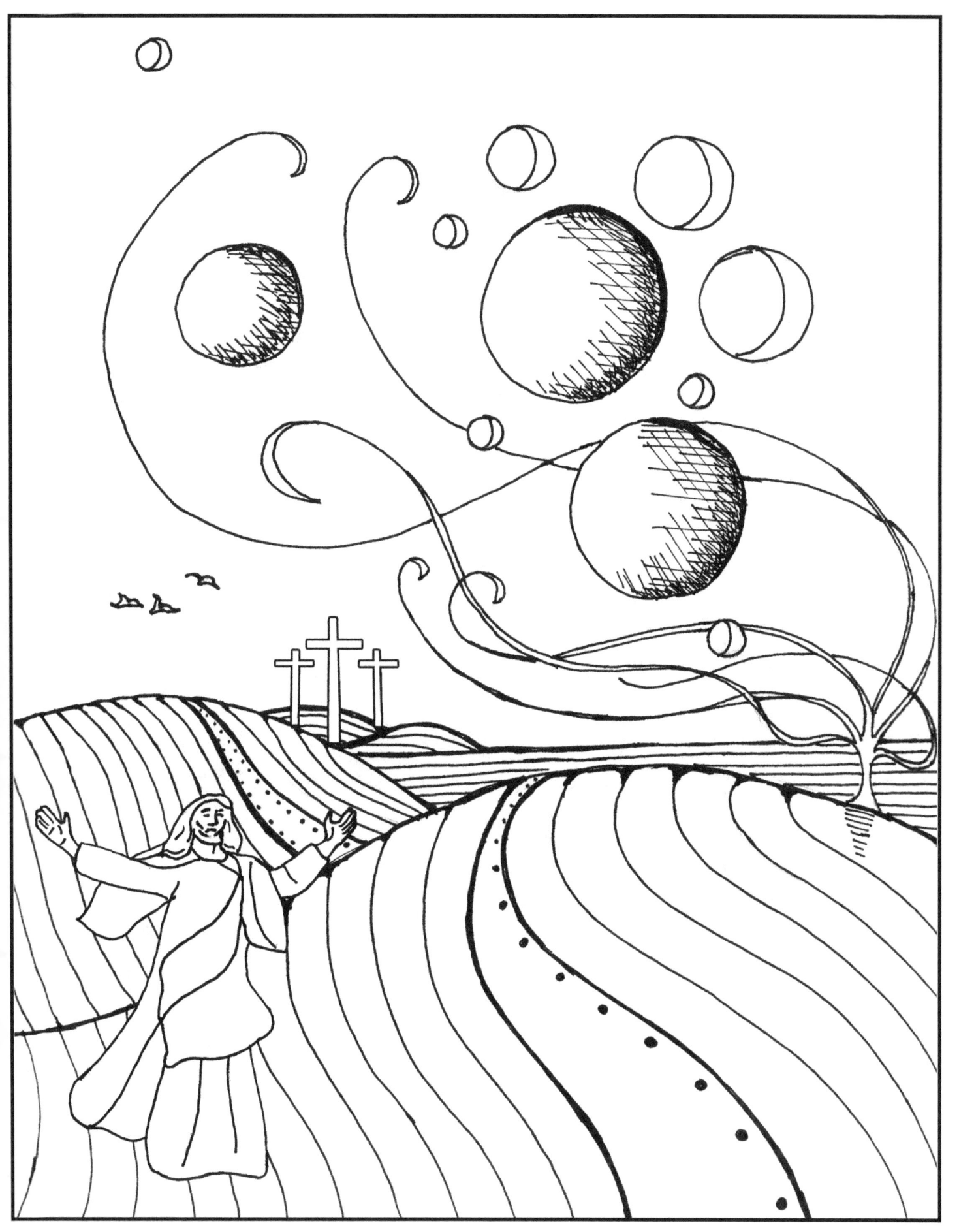

LUKE 24 "JESUS HAS RISEN"

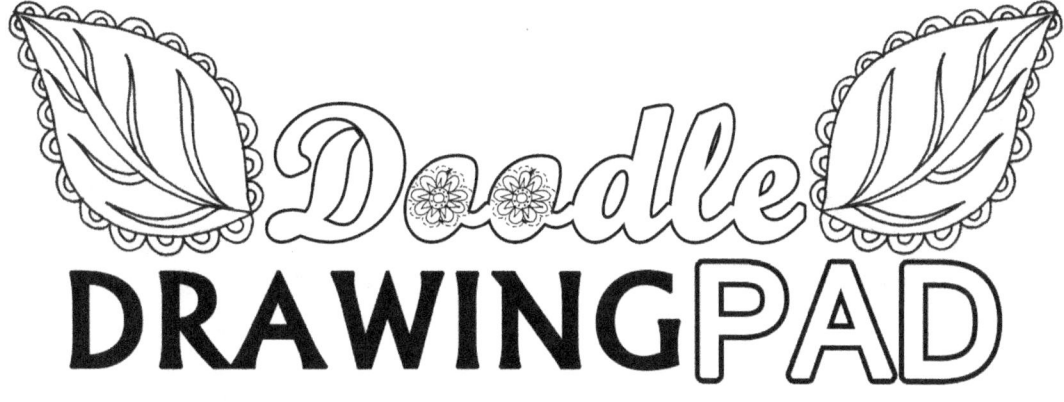

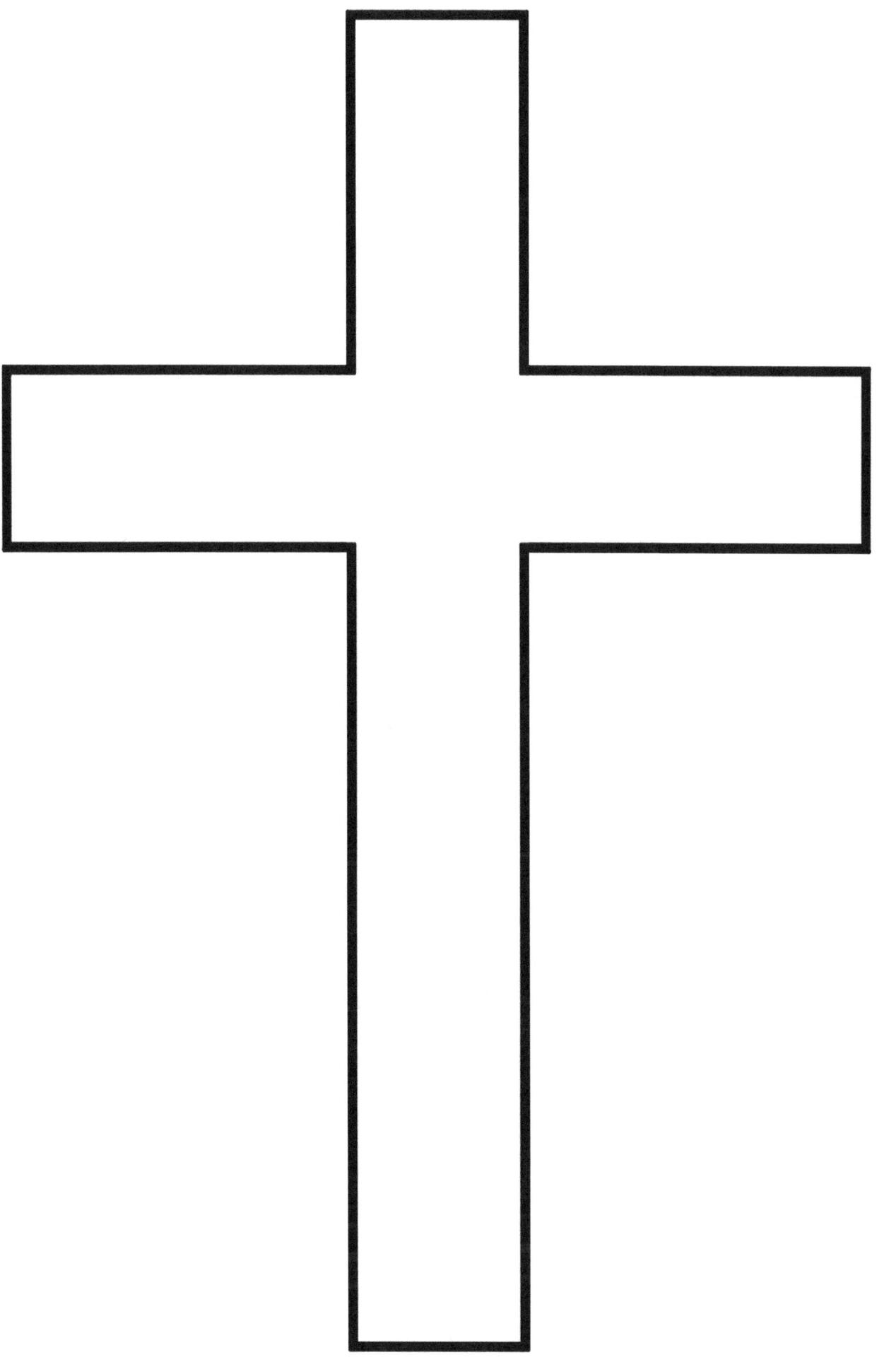

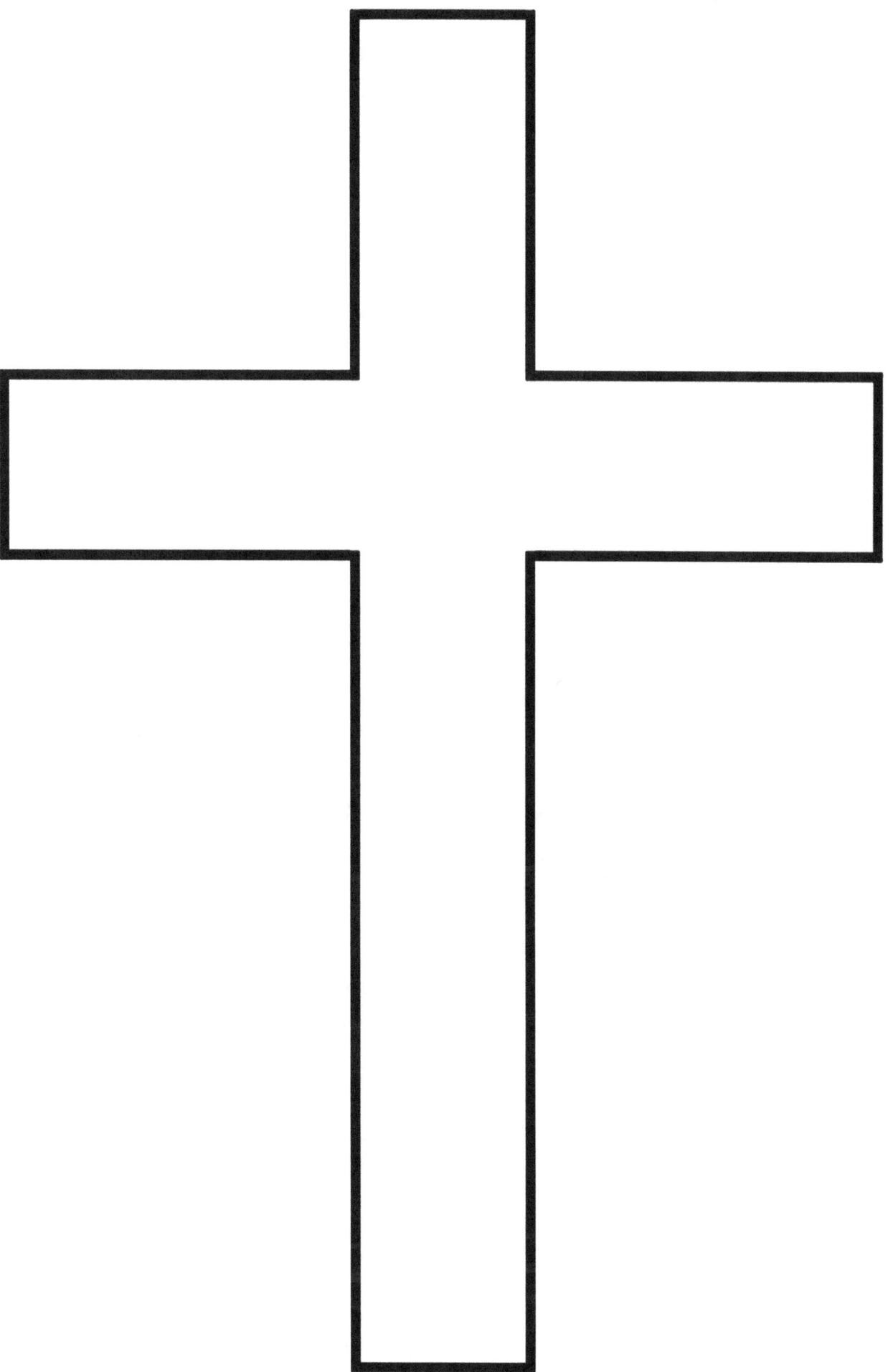

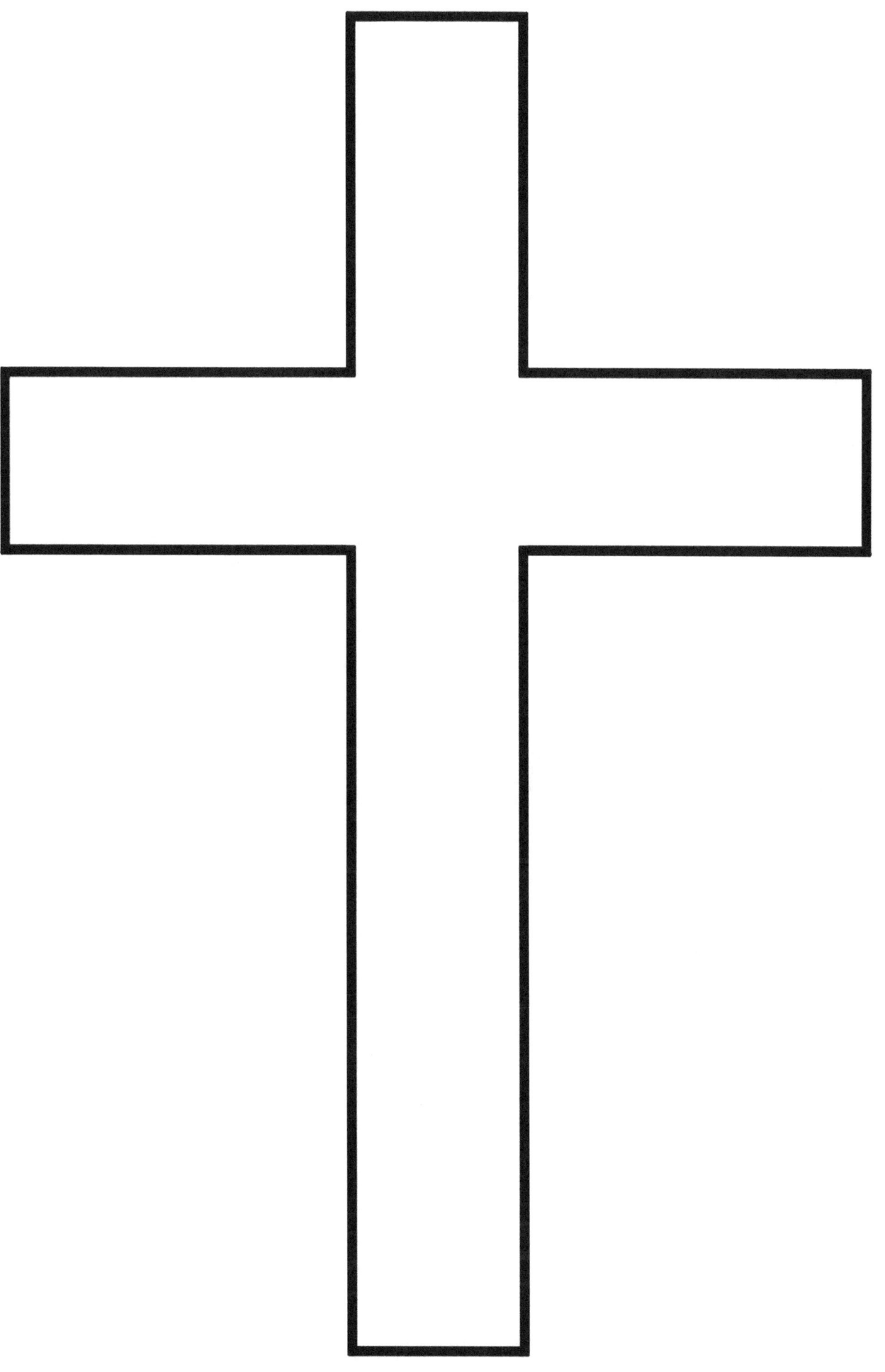

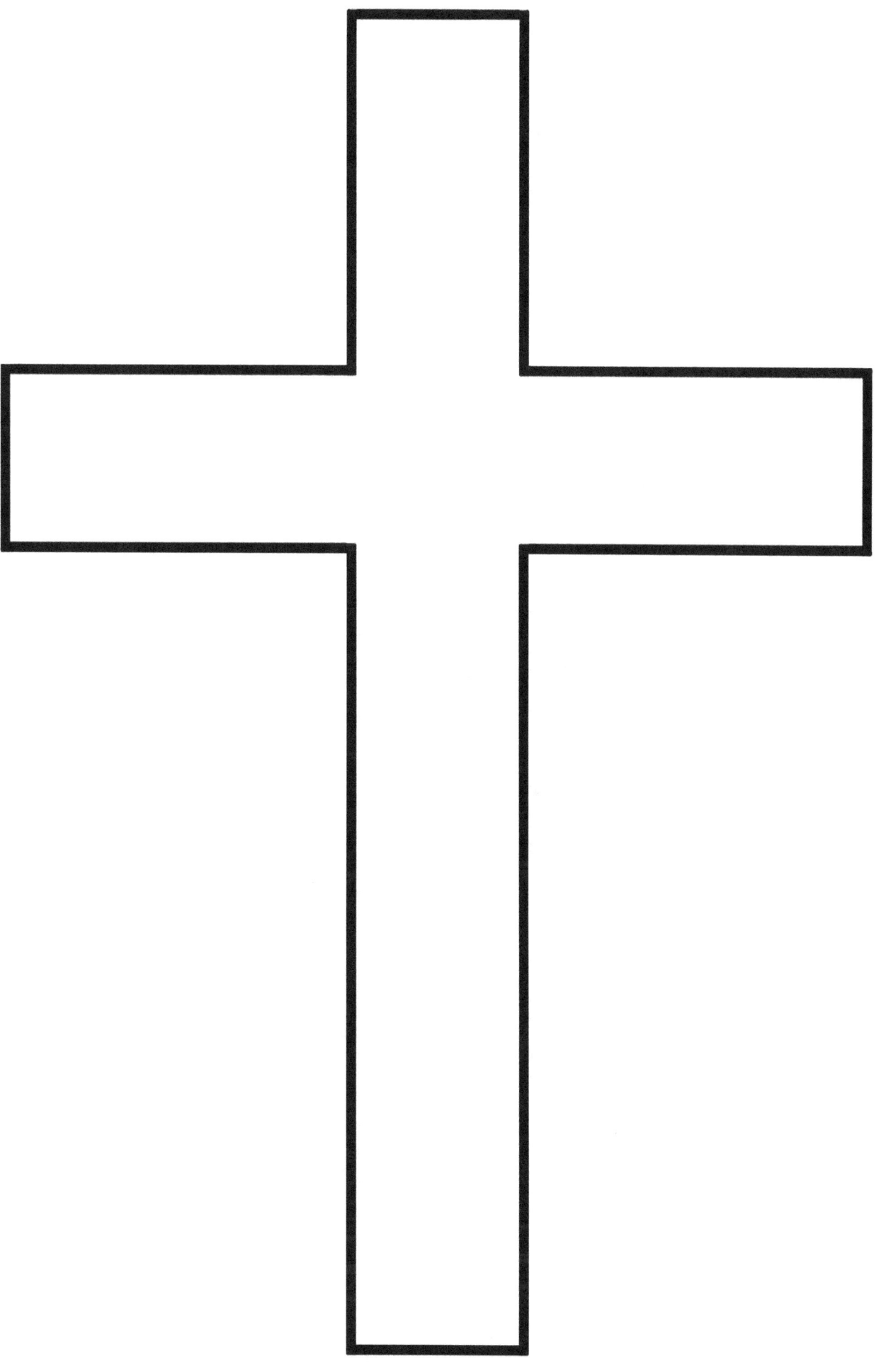

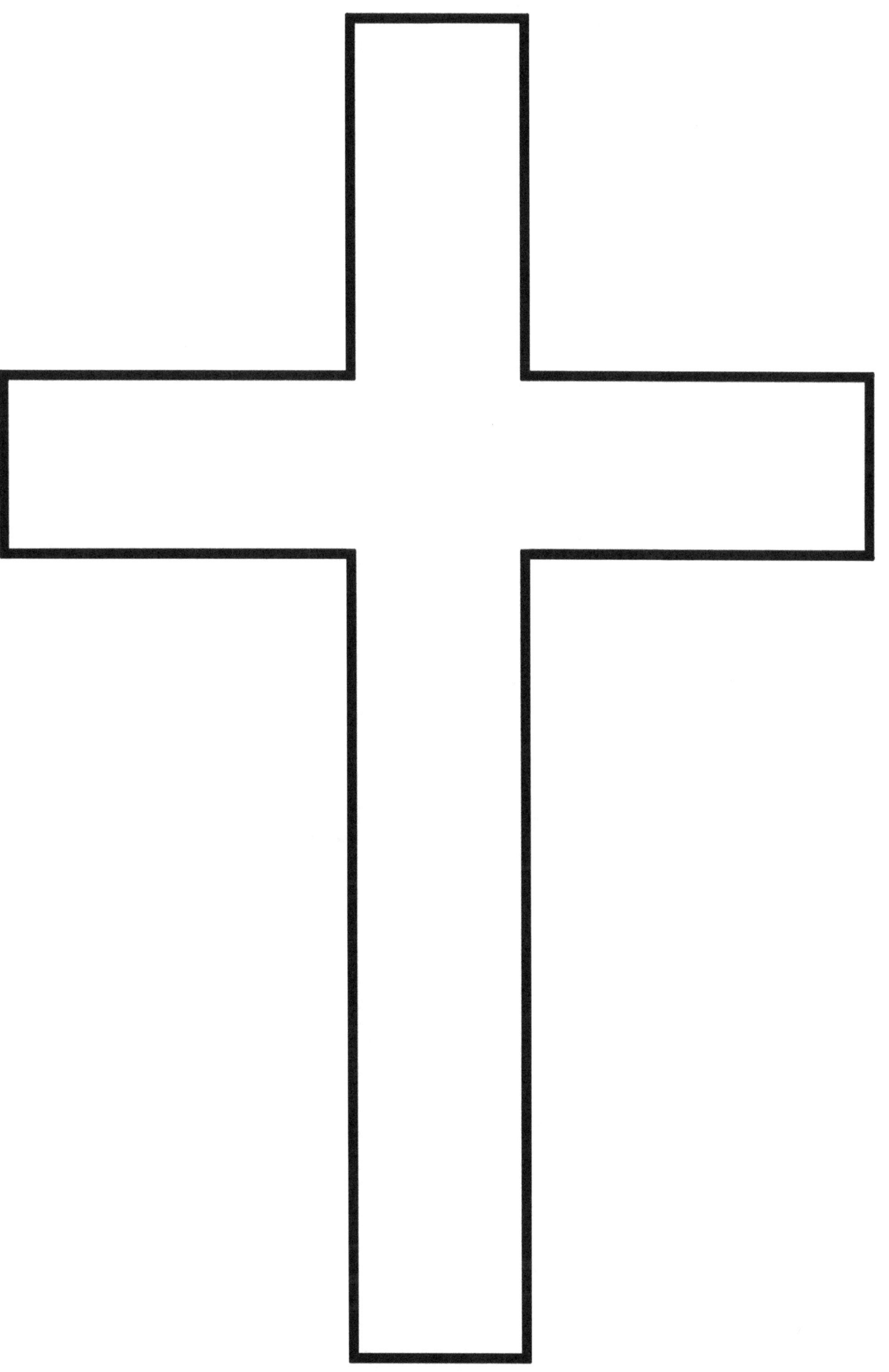

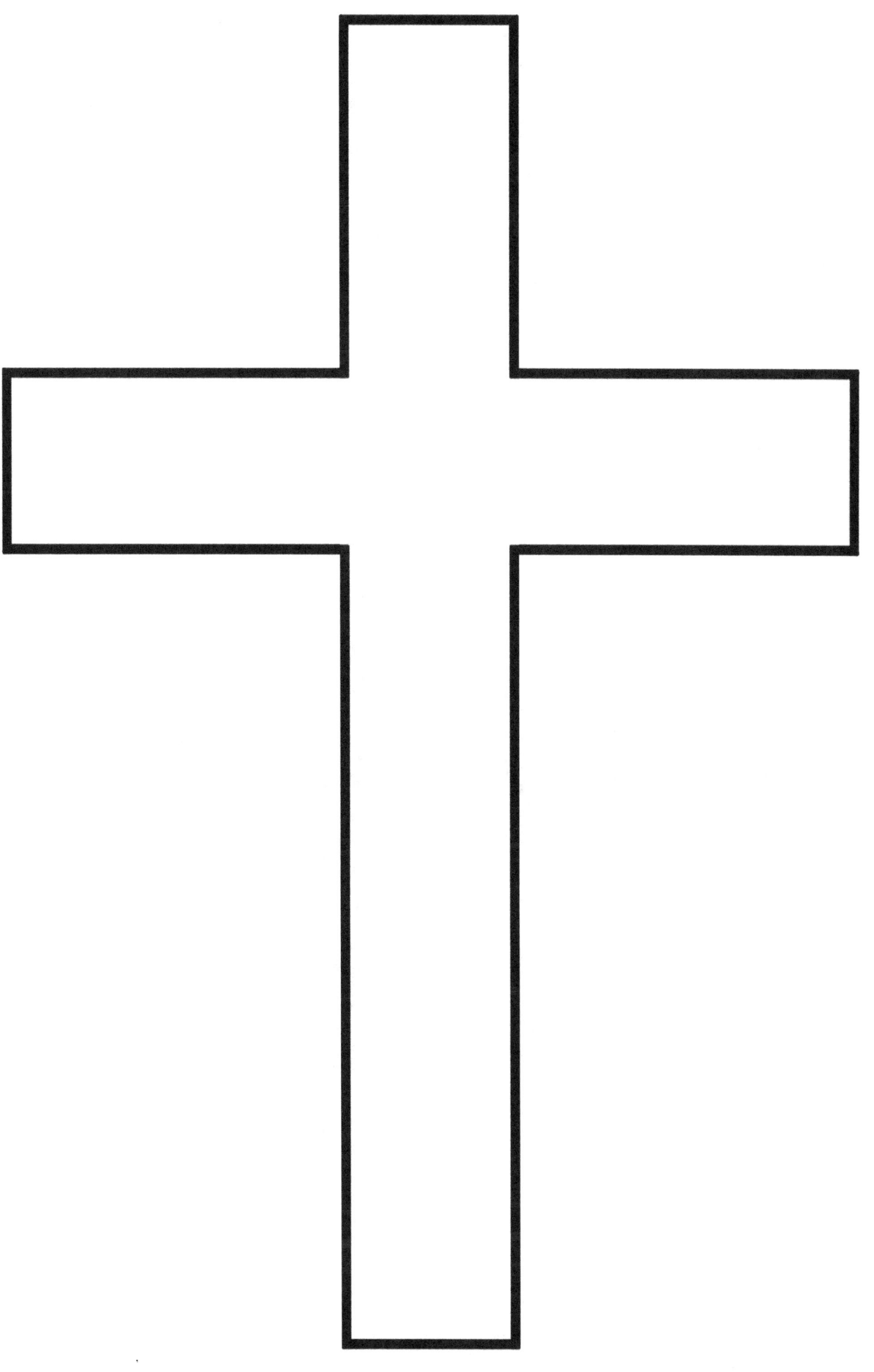

www.ingramcontent.com/pod-product-compliance
Lightning Source LLC
Chambersburg PA
CBHW081313170526
45166CB00011B/3512